Harnessing the Interagency for Complex Operations

Neyla Arnas, Charles Barry, and Robert B. Oakley

Center for Technology and National Security Policy

National Defense University

August 2005

Neyla Arnas is a Senior Research Fellow at the Center for Technology and National Security Policy. Ms. Arnas is a graduate of Louisiana State University and holds a Masters degree in Political Science and Bachelors degrees in Political Science and French. Most recently, Ms. Arnas was the Policy Program Director at the Near East South Asia Center for Strategic Studies. She previously served at the U.S. Department of State as a Speechwriter and Public Affairs Officer to the Director General of the Foreign Service (2000-2004) and Special Advisor in the Bureau of European Affairs (1998-2000) where she focused on European security issues. Ms. Arnas can be contacted at (202) 685-2590, or by email at arnasn@ndu.edu.

Charles Barry is a retired U.S. Army officer associated with NDU since 1993 as a military analyst specializing in transatlantic relations, defense information systems, U.S. grand strategy, and Army force structure. Mr. Barry has been a military strategist for more than 20 years and is considered an expert on strategy, international relations, and information systems related to command and control. He also consults on public sector organizational development, productivity, and resource management. His current areas of concentration include DOD operational network integration, joint stabilization and reconstruction operations, and international capabilities in support of U.S. military operations. Mr. Barry is a doctoral candidate in Public Information Resource Management at the University of Baltimore.

Robert B. Oakley is a Distinguished Research Fellow in the INSS Research Directorate. Ambassador Oakley retired from the Department of State in 1991 after 34 years of diplomatic service. His positions included Ambassador to Pakistan, Zaire, and Somalia; Coordinator for Counterterrorism; Assistant to the President for the Middle East and South Asia on National Security Council staff, and Deputy Assistant Secretary of State for East Asia Affairs. Ambassador Oakley subsequently served President George H. W. Bush and President Bill Clinton as Special Envoy to Somalia.

Defense & Technology Papers *are published by the National Defense University Center for Technology and National Security Policy, Fort Lesley J. McNair, Washington, DC. CTNSP publications are available online at http://www.ndu.edu/ctnsp/publications.html.*

Contents

Introduction[1]

This paper attempts to catalogue and describe the known models for interagency cooperation for stabilization and reconstruction (S&R) operations. The models in existence and under discussion can be grouped in terms of their focus on different aspects of the interagency process, as well as on different aspects of S&R. We recognize that S&R operations take place in an international arena, hence have limited the focus of this paper on models that address how the United States Government (USG) should achieve unity of effort. Defining an efficient, commonly understood model to guide USG actions is a necessary first step to coordinating S&R operations with other international, national, and non-governmental actors.

This paper does not explore the various modes of providing humanitarian assistance, although those activities are almost always important elements of any operation preceding and accompanying military actions, as was seen in Afghanistan and in South Asia with tsunami relief. Humanitarian assistance employs some of the same interagency assets, including the military. The U.S. Agency for International Development (USAID) has the lead to provide humanitarian assistance and has significant resources in material and personnel on call.

The United States has been involved in S&R operations for the past 15 years with mixed success because of the ad hoc nature of pulling together interagency resources. Examples of U.S. S&R efforts include operations in Somalia, Haiti, Bosnia, Kosovo, Afghanistan, and Iraq. A number of ideas have emerged to make the process more systematic. This paper describes those ideas for interagency cooperation, grouping them into three categories: Washington-level strategic cooperation; combatant command-level operational cooperation; and field-level tactical cooperation. Some models address more than one category.

Each section considers recent examples of interagency operations in Iraq and Afghanistan using existing models as well as the use of a Joint Interagency Coordination Group (JIACG) by various Combatant Commanders (COCOMs) before proceeding with a description of proposed new models for cooperation.

S&R—Context of the Interagency Enterprise

Civil-military cooperation on S&R spans pre-conflict planning, training, and deployment, stabilization operations as the conflict unfolds, and post-conflict operations that are

---

[1] This paper is one of several related CTNSP S&R undertakings that address related communications systems and information exchange requirements, Army professional jurisdiction over post-conflict competencies and how the military—principally the Army—should be organized for S&R operations. All of these research projects are interrelated in multiple ways and draw on each other. This cluster of projects builds on CTNSP research conducted in mid-2003 for the Office of the Secretary of Defense, Office of Force Transformation.

expected to unfold unevenly across the operational area as combat operations subside and, at times, re-ignite.

Within the Department of Defense (DOD), cooperation among the military services has evolved painstakingly, beginning with the first Army-Navy Board in 1903 that sought to remedy poor interdepartmental cooperation during the Spanish-American War. Though the National Security Act of 1947 finally brought the services into one federal department, it was not until the 1986 Goldwater-Nichols Act that joint cooperation truly began. Today, military operational jointness is looked to as an example for interagency cooperation on all matters from homeland security to overseas operations. Often overlooked in debates about interagency cooperation is the long arduous path that led to today's military cooperation, which remains a work in progress. By comparison, an integrated interagency process for cooperation in this class of operations is very near its inception.

Fighting and winning wars is more than a military undertaking. It requires achieving political goals that go beyond defeat of an enemy force. Stabilizing countries, assisting traumatized populations, and rebuilding societies and institutions—public and private— are essential to achieving political aims. Immediate stabilization and the establishment of public security are largely but not solely military tasks. Military forces can, with their resources, reconnect some essential services, but their efforts cannot approach the standards required for S&R success without additional assistance, especially over the long term. The notion that combat commanders are able to devote the requisite staff effort to planning and executing S&R tasks while residual combat operations are still going on is flawed. Evidence of this can be seen in recent operations, particularly in Iraq, raising a number of questions. How should interagency cooperation be provided and organized? Should a separate entity be deployed? How would such an entity be staffed, protected, and resourced? Who would execute its policies? When should it arrive?

While these questions have surfaced largely as a result of the situations in Iraq and Afghanistan, it is important to note that S&R operations also can be required completely apart from U.S. combat operations. In these situations the military may still be dominant, because U.S. forces are present in all theaters worldwide and are currently nearly all the government has to draw on for immediate crisis response. Should there be a civilian counterpart to military rapid response capabilities? If so, how should that be done? If not, how should military and civilian skills be brought together into a single, deployable, and effective whole?

Many essential actors are engaged in S&R operations besides the U.S. interagency (DOD included). These must be both represented and well connected systemically to whatever model is employed. Expertise (beyond interagency skills) may be needed to advise on economic, cultural, religious, ethnic, financial, monetary, geographic, commercial, and environmental factors. A model also may need to consider representation from other governments (military and civilian), international organizations (IOs), non-governmental organizations (NGOs), and private volunteer organizations (PVOs). That same model also may need to provide for liaison with local government, civic and business leaders, and local and international contractors.

Among the many questions a successful model must answer, the first will always be, Who should be in charge of S&R operations? What is the authority of the ambassador or the combatant commander over civilian U.S. agencies in a model? Is there a single leader? Are others advisors? Is there a co-leadership situation? Who issues orders, allocates funds, and determines priorities at the operational level, pursuant to U.S. interests and strategies determined by the President?

The question of who should be in charge of U.S. S&R operations is a key facet in assessing the suitability of many models. At the highest strategic level, civilian leadership in the person of the President is readily apparent and universally acknowledged. However, the relationships among other top-level interagency officials are not as clear. In particular, the span of control and authority of both the senior civilian representative—ambassador or President's Special Representative (PSR)—and the senior military commander in the field is often hard to define. Past experience has shown that one cannot be formally subordinate to the other. By law, PSRs have authority over civilian agencies and operations in the field. Until now, relationships primarily have been personality driven. Recent experiences in Afghanistan and Iraq, as well as earlier operations, attest to the importance of good personal relationships. Where they exist, coordination is effective; where they don't, it is problematic. In some situations, the senior civilian authority has taken a supporting role, thereby enhancing coordination.

For some operations it may be possible to appoint an overall civilian leader from the outset, especially for purely humanitarian operations or where a ceasefire or peace agreement is in place. With these scenarios, suitable models should provide for civilian-led interagency efforts at the operational level.

In other situations it will be imperative for the military to lead initial interagency S&R operations because the requirements for early stabilization and initial reconstruction often unfold in ragged ways. Combat operations might continue or have to be renewed because of insurgent actions. The military will need operational interagency support as they restore order, triage post combat uncertainty, and head off instability or anarchy. In such instances military leadership of the initial interagency effort is essential. Suitable models should provide for interagency support to COCOM-led S&R operations for these situations.

Finally, suitable interagency S&R models must be developed for passing overall leadership to civilian control as progress is made toward normal, peacetime, bilateral relations. Deciding when control of an operation should pass from military control to diplomatic leadership should depend on progress made toward the twin goals of executing effective interagency S&R operations and of returning to normal Department of State-led relations as soon as possible.

The most successful interagency model likely will combine elements of several models, as many models address various aspects of coordination from the strategy/policy level through the operational and tactical levels. The most successful model will be the one that merges data from the field with Washington inputs in the most operationally useful manner, drawing on the successes of past experiences while developing more streamlined strategies. Also fundamental to the success of any model is a clear understanding of leadership at each level of cooperation—strategic, operational, and tactical—and clarity of National Security Council (NSC) leadership.

<u>Organizing the Models</u>

The groupings below attempt to provide a framework for analyzing various models for interagency cooperation on S&R, recognizing that some models address concerns that go beyond S&R. Tier One models describe the strategic Washington-based interagency cooperation, including the past and present NSC directives that guide current interagency policymaking. Tier Two models focus mainly on operational interagency cooperation at the COCOM level and include existing mechanisms, the JIACGs, and proposed new models. Tier Three models focus only on formal interagency relationships in the field.

Tier One: Washington-level Cooperation (Strategic)

Existing Efforts

National Security Policy Directive (NSPD) 1[2]

NSPD 1 is the document that establishes the current administration's interagency cooperation methodology. Under NSPD 1, NSC Policy Coordination Committees (NSC/PCCs) are the main day-to-day vehicles for interagency coordination of national security policy. The PCCs are charged with providing policy analysis for consideration by the Principals Committee (PC) and the Deputies Committee (DC) to ensure timely responses to decisions made by the President. The composition of each PCC includes the same representation as the DC.

NSPD 1 establishes six regional PCCs chaired by an Under Secretary or Assistant Secretary rank official designated by the Secretary of State. It also establishes 11 functional PCCs chaired by an Under Secretary or Assistant Secretary rank official designated by various authorities according to the topic. Each PCC has an Executive Secretary from the NSC staff who assists the Chairman in agenda setting, task assignment, and responding to the PCs/DCs.

Presidential Decision Directive (PDD) 56[3]

This model was used during the Clinton Administration and called on the DC to establish interagency working groups to develop, plan, and execute contingency operations. The DC would form an Executive Committee (ExCom) to supervise the day-to-day management of U.S. engagement. The ExCom would bring together representatives of all appropriate agencies.

The DC would task the development of a political-military plan and assign specific responsibilities to ExCom officials. Each ExCom official would be required to develop their respective part of the plan in full coordination among relevant agencies. This model also called for a rehearsal of the political-military plan conducted by the DC where the ExCom officials would present their supporting agency plans to ensure a seamless operation.

The final two elements of the plan are an after action review directed by the ExCom and the development of an interagency training program.

---

[2] The White House, "Organization of the National Security Council System," February 13, 2001.
[3] PDD 56, May 1997.

National Security Planning Directive (NSPD) XX[4]

This model, still in draft, was designed to replace the PDD 56 model. It creates a Contingency Planning Policy Coordination Committee (PCC) which would meet monthly to assess intelligence reports to determine areas of potential concern. This committee would work closely with a regional PCC. Together they would report issues and recommendations to the DC in quarterly briefings. The principals and DC would oversee the development of strategy, as well as the implementation of actions. The National Security Advisor (NSA), through the Contingency Planning PCC, would coordinate all interagency planning activities.

Military planning is delegated to a contingency planning sub-group chaired by the NSC Senior Director for Defense Policy and Arms Control.

Iraq Experience[5]

Washington-based interagency engagement during the preparation for war with Iraq generally followed procedures established in NSPD 1. However, consistent with U.S. war planning tradition, interagency coordination was more supportive than directive in the main war planning effort which centered at the Pentagon. Issues were considered and coordinated by PCCs, DCs and PCs, all with the objective of ensuring support of the lead agency, DOD, as represented by both the Office of the Secretary of Defense (OSD) and the Joint Staff.

With regard to S&R planning, responsibility for both planning and execution resided with OSD and its designated director for the post conflict phase, LTG Jay W. Garner, USA (ret.). NSPD 24 established the Office of Reconstruction and Humanitarian Affairs (ORHA) and defined its objectives. Broadly speaking, ORHA had two mandates: to provide humanitarian assistance and facilitate reconstruction operations. Once ORHA deployed to the field, its subordinate organization changed and its mandates grew in number to include: addressing humanitarian assistance; reconstruction of Iraqi infrastructure; establishing civilian administration/governance; and providing for its own operational needs. The PCC meetings mainly addressed the personnel staffing issues of ORHA. In the six weeks before deploying the field, ORHA developed into an organization of 167 interagency people (65 -70 military and the rest civilian). By the time it transitioned to the Coalition Provisional Authority (CPA), it numbered more than 1,100. In retrospect, the insular planning within DOD failed to vet fully potential gaps in S&R requirements, both in terms of substance and process. The primary focus of DOD was on winning the war and only secondarily (or subsequently) on securing post-war Iraq.

---

[4] NSPD XX: Anticipating, Preventing, and Responding to Complex Foreign Crises. It is designated "XX" as it is still awaiting presidential signature.
[5] Paul Hughes, Chief of Special Initiatives Office for ORHA and Chief of Strategic Policy for CPA, January-August 2003. Personal interview, Washington, DC, April 4, 2005.

<u>Office of the Coordinator for Reconstruction and Stabilization (S/CRS) Operations</u>[6]

The S/CRS established in the DOS is in the process of developing the construct for how it would lead the civilian component of S&R cooperation. While none of the institutional parts are yet in place, the NSC has approved the notion of Country Reconstruction and Stabilization Groups (CRSG). The primary functions of a CRSG would be strategic planning, policy coordination, and resource allocation. S/CRS would embody the strategic management of S&R operations through the CRSGs, reporting directly to the NSC Deputies Committee. A CRSG would be organized for all DOD contingency plans and would be activated for exercises and in the run up to actual operations. The CRSG members would be taken from permanent PCCs co-chaired by S/CRS and NSC reps. Committee competencies include governance, economic stabilization, humanitarian assistance, resource management, and infrastructure.

Proposed Efforts

<u>Center for Strategic and International Studies (CSIS) Model</u>[7]

The CSIS model is a new proposal and calls for strengthening interagency integration mechanisms at all levels—in Washington, in the regions, and in the field. At the strategic level, the CSIS model creates an NSC Senior Director and office for Complex Contingency Planning to lead the development of integrated interagency plans for complex contingency operations, including S&R operations. Planning offices are established in each of the key civilian agencies (in State, this would be S/CRS) to participate in the interagency planning process. The CSIS model calls for NSC standard operating procedures (similar to PDD-56 and NSPD XX) for interagency planning and oversight for complex operations.

<u>Defense Science Board (DSB) Model</u>[8]

The DSB Model proposes establishing cross-government contingency planning and integration task forces for countries "ripe and important" under the leadership and direction of the president or NSC. Task force membership would include representation from all involved USG agencies. Task force strategic plans would be supported by "component" plans prepared by the regional combatant commanders, thus better integrating S&R plans with operational plans for combat.

---

[6] The description of S/CRS is based on information provided to the authors in March and April 2005. S/CRS continues to refine its concepts.

[7] Michele Flournoy, Senior Advisor, CSIS International Security Program. Co-author of *Winning the Peace: An American Strategy for Post-Conflict Reconstruction*, CSIS, 2004. Email interview, March 2005.

[8] Office of the Under Secretary of Defense for Acquisition, Technology, and Logistics, "Transition to and from Hostilities," December 2004. Available online at: <http://www.acq.osd mil/dsb/reports/2004-12-DSB_SS_Report_Final.pdf>. This document is considered the basis for the current draft directive on "DOD Capabilities for Stability Operations."

The decision to launch aggressive interagency planning and actions would come from the president or NSC—they also would determine the leadership of the task forces. These government-wide planning and integration task forces would report to the NSC. Several of them could be underway concurrently.

This model further suggests that the Secretaries of Defense and State jointly propose a NSPD to assign specific roles and responsibilities to various departments and agencies as well as make explicit the NSC role in managing national resources for crisis planning. A small, permanent cadre within the NSC staff would provide continuity and expertise for long-term issues.

Tier Two: COCOM-level Cooperation (Operational)

Existing Efforts

Iraq Experience[9]

Once ORHA deployed to Kuwait, all its operational needs, for example lodging, communications, and transportation, were contracted out. During the five weeks spent in Kuwait prior to entering Baghdad, ORHA coordinated with the NGOs and embassies of other countries principally to address anticipated humanitarian relief issues while also creating a detailed plan for ministry advisory teams that would focus on continuing the day-to-day operations of the various Iraqi ministries. General Garner's coordination with GEN Tommy R. Franks, Commander of U.S. Central Command (CENTCOM), whose focus was on the war and not on post-conflict issues, was limited by the CENTCOM decision to place ORHA in a quasi-subordinate role to the Coalition Forces Land Component Command (CFLCC). Because of this organizational relationship, coordination for support and synchronization of efforts between ORHA and the military staffs of both CFLCC and CENTCOM were inefficient and disjointed. The lack of co-location of the two leaders did not help the situation nor did their different priorities. General Franks was at his forward headquarters in Qatar while General Garner was in Kuwait and later Iraq; both reported separately to the Pentagon; one was focused on rebuilding Iraq while the other was still trying to win the war. Developing an interagency perspective was not a priority within the Pentagon, nor with the combatant commander, and was made more difficult once the players deployed to the field.

Joint Interagency Coordination Groups (JIACGs) at the COCOMs[10]

Since May 2000, U.S. Joint Forces Command (JFCOM) has been working on a prototype to enhance interagency planning and coordination at the operational level. In response to 9/11, the regional COCOMs expressed an immediate need for coordination on counterterrorism issues within the interagency. In response to this need and based on JFCOM's on-going work, the NSC established in March 2002 a "limited capability" JIACG in each regional command. This approval came with three DOD-funded positions for representatives from Treasury, State, and Justice at each COCOM.

Each COCOM has used the "limited" JIACG differently. No two JIACGs look or operate alike. In the absence of formal structures, the various COCOMs developed their own constructs. For example, in some cases, the JIACG reports to the J-3, in others, to the Deputy Commander. The leadership within a JIACG has been driven by the COCOMs'

---

[9] Paul Hughes, Chief of Special Initiatives Office for ORHA and Chief of Strategic Policy for CPA, January-August 2003. Personal interview, Washington, DC, April 4, 2005.

[10] COL Matthew Bogdanos, CENTCOM. Portions of this section were adapted from "Joint Interagency Coordination Groups: The First Steps," *Joint Force Quarterly*, April 2005.

needs. Overall, the current "limited" JIACGs' focus on counterterrorism and counter narcotics issues has proven valuable and all of the COCOMs have expressed interest in going "full-spectrum." The lay-out of each JIACG is discussed in more detail below.

1. U.S. Central Command (CENTCOM) JIACG

Owing to Operations *Enduring Freedom* and *Iraqi Freedom*, CENTCOM established the first and largest JIACG (for counterterrorist activities) and conducted split-based operations from CENTCOM headquarters in Tampa, Florida, and Qatar. They also deployed more than 90 military and civilian personnel to Afghanistan in 2001 and sent a similar number to Iraq in 2003.

Afghanistan: Initially operating more as a task force, the CENTCOM JIACG was deployed to Afghanistan in November 2001 with members from the Federal Bureau of Investigation (FBI), Central Intelligence Agency (CIA), Diplomatic Security Service (DSS), U.S. Customs Service, National Security Agency, Defense Intelligence Agency (DIA), Defense Human Intelligence Service, New York's Joint Terrorism Task Force, DOS, and the Justice and Treasury Departments, among others. Through a small detachment in Tampa, the CENTCOM JIACG established and maintained real-time communications from the field to Washington, functioning primarily as an intelligence-gathering fusion center, while at the same time jointly operating Afghanistan's main interrogation facility in Bagram.

Iraq: After Afghanistan, the CENTCOM JIACG began to transform from an operation-specific task force into a comprehensive JIACG better able to wage the long-term war on terrorism. Adding representatives from the Department of Energy, the Treasury Department Office of Foreign Assets Control (OFAC), the Defense Threat Reduction Agency (DTRA), the Internal Revenue Service (IRS), and the DOS International Information Programs, JIACG maintained small detachments in Tampa and in CENTCOM forward headquarters in Qatar. However, in March 2003 the majority of its personnel deployed to Iraq in task-organized teams to search for evidence identifying terrorist-financing networks and terrorist activity in the United States, to investigate UN Security Council Resolution violations, and to initiate criminal investigations of U.S. and foreign individuals who assisted Iraq with its weapons of mass destruction (WMD) programs.

Current Status: The CENTCOM JIACG operates as an independent staff that reports to the deputy commander through the chief of staff, thereby ensuring unity of effort among the individual staff directorates that might otherwise view interagency issues from their limited and sometimes competing perspectives. Such senior leadership also has enhanced the direct coordination with senior-level non-DOD representatives necessary for JIACG operations. Its current mission is to support other directorates in four functional areas—political-military (or ambassadorial) activities, civil-military operations, intelligence fusion, and CIA-specific operational advice—while taking the lead on counterterrorism-related initiatives within the law-enforcement community. It continues to provide support to subordinate forces throughout its area of operations, to include a robust presence in

Iraq and Afghanistan of both interagency-trained liaison officers and task-organized teams of varying size.

Both the Director and Deputy Director of the CENTCOM JIACG have always been military personnel. Under the Chairman's guidance, DOD cannot task representatives of other agencies. In order to address the issue of command in a combat zone, all members of the CENTCOM JIACG have agreed that each agency headquarters retains tasking authority (in DOD terms, operational control) of their deployed members, but that the senior JIACG military member in the field has direction and control of all movements necessary to accomplish whatever tasks are assigned (in DOD terms, tactical control) of those members. In order to achieve consensus and overall direction on its interagency activities, CENTCOM also has established an interagency executive steering committee to function as an operational-level PCC. Chaired by the deputy commander; co-chaired by the command's political adviser; and staffed by the command's directors, senior DOD, and other agency representatives; this committee guides the command's interagency policy, reviews and initiates major interagency proposals, and manages competing priorities. Effective July 1, 2005, the Director position will be held by a Senior Executive Service (SES)-level civilian.

2. U.S. European Command (EUCOM) JIACG

The EUCOM JIACG is a division within the EUCOM Plans and Operations Center (their Standing Joint Force Headquarters) and initially focused on counterterrorism. The EUCOM JIACG comprises national agency representatives and a military staff functioning as a de-facto Joint Interagency Coordination Center. Representatives from the DOS Counterterrorism Section, FBI, and Office of Foreign Assets Control (OFAC) reside within the JIACG structure, while the command's Political Advisor, DSS liaison officer, DTRA representative, and the representatives of various national intelligence agencies participate and collaborate under their broader mission charter. The EUCOM Commander has provisionally expanded the JIACG mission to include "full-spectrum" activity in order to meet theater security cooperation and defense transformation demands in Africa, Europe, and Eurasia. Their greatest current challenge is orchestrating collaborative interagency planning at the theater-regional level with the non-resident U.S. and non-U.S. governmental agencies, NGOs, PVOs, and academic institutions to meet this expanded role.

3. U.S. Pacific Command (PACOM) JIACG

Immediately after 9/11, PACOM established its Joint Inter-Agency Coordination Group Combating Terrorism (JIACG/CT) and designated it to be the PACOM Office of Primary Responsibility for the Global War on Terrorism (GWOT). Its responsibilities have evolved over time and now include Transnational Crimes, WMD Proliferation Security, and Regional Maritime Security. Charged with creating an architecture to enable and ensure robust coordination within the PACOM area of responsibility (AOR) at the operational level among U.S. agencies and Embassies, and regional governments and organizations, the PACOM JIACG has developed a number of protocols and procedures within the Command and relationships with agencies outside the command, notably DOS. These include drafting a Combating Terrorism (CT) Campaign Plan for coordinating and directing the Command's traditional activities (intelligence production, training, security assistance, security cooperation) and coordinating the development of a concept of regional maritime security with the Asian Regional Forum.

JIACG/CT began with a budget of $2 million and 35 personnel reassigned from within the command. Located within the J3 directorate, JIACG/CT reports to the Director for Operations, has 18 military personnel (although only ten are in authorized military billets), and is led by a military O-6 Chief. Members also include one government-service (GS) employee, six contractors, two Liaison Officers (LNOs) from the command, and representatives from DOS and the Treasury Department. An FBI agent officer is scheduled to arrive, and negotiations are underway with USAID. Nevertheless, JIACG/CT efforts have been consistently threatened by staff and resource restrictions.

4. NORAD-U.S. Northern Command (NORTHCOM) JIACG

The NORAD-USNORTHCOM (N-NC) Joint Interagency Coordination Group (JIACG) is the Commander's primary interagency forum. Its mission is to integrate and synchronize interagency activities to ensure mutual understanding, unity of effort, and full spectrum support to and from NORAD and USNORTHCOM. The foundation of the JIACG is an Interagency Coordination Directorate, led by an SES Director who supports all JIACG related operations, exercises, plans, and initiatives for the commands. JIACG membership includes representatives of all staff elements, components, COCOM LNOs, and interagency partners. Currently approximately 60 agencies have assigned resident representatives to the JIACG while more than 100 agencies collaborate remotely. The JIACG is not a separate staff and coordination process, but rather facilitates and becomes a "force multiplier" to the existing command and staff process. JIACG agency representatives and LNOs provide the interagency subject matter expertise and reach back to parent agencies and commands that are critical for mutual support of both Homeland Defense (HLD) and Homeland Security (HLS) missions. Day to day, agency members sit in the various directorates that benefit the most from daily synchronization. Twice a month the JIACG formally meets for education, team building, and to discuss working group issues. During contingency and exercise periods, the Intelligence Community (IC) Directorate forms a centralized synchronization cell to support the JIACG in reaching across the command elements to maximize the potential for interagency coordination at all levels.

5. U.S. Strategic Command (STRATCOM) JAICG

The STRATCOM JIACG is designed to maintain links with civilian agencies, support the command's deliberate planning processes, support global operations and crisis-action planning activities, and participate in training and exercises. Reporting to the Deputy Commander, its Director is the command Deputy Political Advisor, a military 0-6. Because so many agencies already reside at STRATCOM (CIA, Defense Advanced Research Projects Agency, Defense Energy Support Center, Defense Information

Systems Agency, DIA, DTRA, Department of Energy, Department of Homeland Security, DOS, Missile Defense Agency, National Aeronautics and Space Administration, National Geospatial-Intelligence Agency, National Reconnaissance Office and the National Security Agency), the greatest challenge is to develop strategic concepts and methodologies through which multiple agencies would be able to agree on desired end states, objectives, and effects. Because STRATCOM was given the lead in January 2005 for combating WMD, this may become the primary mission of the JIACG.

6. U.S. Transportation Command (TRANSCOM) JIACG

The TRANSCOM JIACG serves as an advisory group to the Commander and his staff, as well as to component commands. Operating across the full spectrum and reporting to the Chief of Staff, the JIACG comprises 20 resident national agency representatives and service LNOs focused on the TRANSCOM global military distribution and transportation mission. The recent designation of TRANSCOM as the DOD Distribution Process Owner has further refined this focus. While the purely volunteer nature of membership in the JIACG has presented unique challenges, the JIACG continues to capitalize on training and building relationships to identify and optimize every opportunity for TRANSCOM and the interagency community to collaborate in efforts to enhance national safety and security.

7. U.S. Southern Command (SOUTHCOM) JIACG

The SOUTHCOM JIACG is a multi-functional advisory staff established under the J-7 Transformation Directorate consisting of two Interagency Specialists. The SOUTHCOM JIACG facilitates coordination, enhances information sharing, and integrates planning efforts between SOUTHCOM and the interagency community. The JIACG establishes habitual collaboration and coordination links and provides interagency advice to deliberate and crisis action planning efforts, as well as for theater engagement plans. Improved coordination is achieved through a combination of regular interagency meetings that include all of the interagency representatives assigned to the command and monthly interagency seminars on relevant topics. The JIACG is being designed to coordinate the full-spectrum of SOUTHCOM operations. The SOUTHCOM JIACG will consist of approximately four military or civilian members, one or two contractors, and one representative each from the Bureau of Alcohol, Tobacco, and Firearms (ATF); Customs; Border Patrol; FBI; DOS and Treasury OFAC either as full time or part time representatives. The SOUTHCOM JIACG also will include (IA) LNOs currently assigned to the SOUTHCOM Headquarters.

Proposed Efforts

JFCOM Full-Spectrum JIACG Concept[11]

As envisioned by JFCOM, a "full-spectrum" JIACG would be a full-time permanent planning and advisory body to the COCOM, owned and reporting to him or her. Essentially, the JFCOM-proposed JIACG would be the COCOM "country team," but at the regional level. For country specific expertise, the JIACG would coordinate with the actual Embassy country team. The JIACG would be a support element for theater engagement; crises and transition planning; and would keep the COCOM staff apprised of the activities of other civilian departments. Decision-making authority would remain with the COCOM. A full spectrum JIACG envisions a physical core group with virtual "add-ons" as needed. The core group would consist of those departments and agencies relevant to the particular COCOM mission, potentially DOS, USAID, Commerce, Treasury, and Justice. Energy and Agriculture also may be part of the core group. The physical members of the JIACG would be limited to those departments necessary to the mission on a full-time basis. The virtual add-ons would "join" the JIACG via collaborative computer tools, allowing different sets of expertise to be brought in on an "as needed" basis and a more elastic group of players. The Director would be a civilian SES planner with interagency experience. Who this would be and which agency the Director would come from would be decided by each COCOM. In some instances, it may be the Political Advisor (POLAD), a DOS-appointee of ambassador or counselor rank who serves on all COCOM staffs; in others, a senior OSD representative (a senior OSD SES billet has been approved for the CENTCOM JIACG). The JIACG Director would be part of the COCOM inner circle, equivalent to the POLAD and J-code directors.

JFCOM has developed this model of a physical/virtual JIACG over a four to five year period and has demonstrated its viability through testing in exercises and operational environments. The unique combination allows a COCOM to garner any manner of expertise on a part-time, as needed, evolving basis.

How a JIACG would coordinate with U.S. embassies in the region would be dependent on the situation and driven by the COCOM. The COCOM also would determine whether or not parts of a JIACG would deploy to the field during a crisis. Interface by the JIACG with Washington would be limited to members' liaisons back to their respective Departments.

During the numerous war games JFCOM undertook with interagency participation, the POLADs unanimously felt that they should not be a part of the JIACG. They viewed POLAD participation in the JIACG as undermining their unique role to the COCOM. As of now, the nature of the POLAD-JIACG interface will be left up to each COCOM.

---

[11] Phil Kearley, J-9, JFCOM. Personal interview, Norfolk, VA, February 10, 2005.

JFCOM views the S/CRS construct as complementary to the JIACG concept. When in time of crisis S/CRS activates its Humanitarian, Reconstruction and Stabilization Team (HRST) planners and sends them to a COCOM, the JIACG would facilitate the integration of the HRST planning efforts. The HRSTs are envisioned as planners who can commit resources (unlike a JIACG). The JIACG would provide situational awareness only.

JFCOM views the CSIS model as a larger model within which the JIACG would fit as the COCOM component. JFCOM also recognizes that the JIACG serves the needs of DOD broadly, and the COCOM specifically. As such, each COCOM has priorities which may not be representative of all USG priorities.

S/CRS Model

The second organizational level of the S/CRS model foresees a HRST. An HRST— approximately six to eight planners, mainly from S/CRS, with appropriate expertise— would deploy for 6 to12 months to the responsible COCOM and assist the COCOM staff in drafting the S&R portion of the military plan. The HRST would report to both the CRSG and the COCOM. The HRST is the only designated planning entity in the S/CRS model. In developing operational S&R plans with the COCOM staff, the HRST would reach back to the CRSG for policy guidance. In turn, the HRST plan would ultimately be executed by Advance Civilian Teams (ACTs), deployed in theater with COCOM military units, from Joint Task Force (JTF) to brigade level.

CSIS Model

At the operational or regional level, the CSIS model seeks both to strengthen interagency coordination and establish a truly interagency contingency planning process. It recommends holding quarterly NSC-chaired interagency "summits" in each region to integrate policy execution across the USG and to focus attention on using all instruments of national power to shape the regional environment and prevent future crises and threats. Each summit would bring together the key USG players in a given region: the NSC Senior Director for the Region (as chair), the COCOM, the Assistant Secretary of State for the region, counterparts from other civilian agencies, and the relevant country ambassadors, among others. In addition, the CSIS model would create rapidly deployable Interagency Crisis Action Teams, chaired by NSC staff with representation from all of the relevant civilian agencies, to lead a truly interagency planning process at the operational level. These teams would work intensively with COCOM planners, but would report to the NSC, not to the COCOM.

Super POLAD Model[12]

The POLAD is typically supported by a two to three person administrative staff. The POLAD's traditional mission is to provide day-to-day political advice to the four star commander and the COCOM staff. The Super POLAD model for post conflict reconstruction elaborates the POLAD's role and expands their jurisdiction to coordinate the full interagency effort supporting the COCOM during pre-conflict planning for S&R, as well as during the execution of post-conflict S&R mission tasks. As execution of S&R operations often occurs in parallel with combat operations—before, during and after a conflict, the POLAD may be assigned a mission even when the COCOM itself has not been involved in the conflict as a combatant.

Under the Super POLAD model, the POLAD would be selected from among the top tier of Foreign Service officers, would be of ambassador rank, and would be designated as a Deputy Assistant Secretary of State for the region. The Super POLADs would have dual reporting channels to both the Combatant Commander and to the Regional Assistant Secretary in Washington. A Super POLAD would oversee interagency planning and actual support to the COCOM by leading a staff comprised of interagency representatives. The Super POLAD's supporting staff would also include requisite expertise in relevant disciplines, such as regional economics, geography, societies, religions, humanitarian operations, financing, ethnicities, and law. The Super POLAD would be equipped to participate in the data flow and communications systems of the interagency as well as appropriate international bodies involved in crisis response. The POLAD also would act as the commander's interface with non-DOD support across the USG, and as the conduit to DOS for political and diplomatic direction. Depending on the situation as the country is stabilized, the POLAD may also become the link to the U.S. ambassador as an embassy is established and the military command falls under traditional civilian control for U.S. bilateral affairs, including military affairs.

Marine Forces Pacific Crisis Management Group (CMG) Model[13]

The concept of a CMG creates a full-time standing organization that can support crisis prevention and crisis response at the operational level, integrating plans before, during, or after a major contingency while providing a cohesive transition from DOD to DOS oversight. This civil-military organization designed to plan, coordinate, and execute the entire range of S&R operations organizes itself along functional lines of operation (diplomacy, security, humanitarian assistance, governance, rule of law, civil administration, economic development, information, human rights, and social reconciliation) rather than typical military style staff lines.

---

[12] This model is an elaboration of the construct outlined in the CTNSP study, *Transforming for Stabilization and Reconstruction Operations,* Hans Binnendijk and Stuart E. Johnson, editors (Washington, DC: National Defense University Press, 2004), pp. 61-64.

[13] Center for Emerging Threats and Opportunities, "Quick Look Report: Interagency Planning and Coordination Models," April 2005. CETO is a think tank dedicated to developing new ideas for the US Marine Corps and is a division of the Marine Corps Warfighting Laboratory.

J-10 Model[14]

The J-10 model envisions a senior political appointee from OSD designated to act as the COCOM representative for interagency affairs and to coordinate interagency planning and oversee interagency support to the command. The J-10 would be a new staff Directorate on each COCOM staff.

OSD unsuccessfully attempted to have the J-10 concept incorporated into the unified command plan process. The J-10 proposal was seen as a variation of the JIACG, with little substantive difference. The proposal is no longer under consideration.

OSD Defense Advisor Model[15]

Following the demise of the J-10 plan numerous alternatives were proposed on how best to incorporate OSD into the COCOMs. Assigning an OSD defense advisor to each COCOM was suggested. The unresolved issue is whether the OSD advisor would work for and report to the COCOM or the Secretary of Defense. The difference between this model and the J-10 concept is that the J-10 concept envisioned the OSD advisor as the leader of an interagency group, whereas in the OSD model, the advisor is the equivalent of an OSD POLAD who would provide policy guidance to the COCOM. This proposal is no longer under consideration.

---

[14] CAPT Charles Neary, J-5. Telephone interview, Washington, DC, February 2005.
[15] Ibid

Tier Three: Field Cooperation (Tactical)

Existing Efforts

Afghanistan Experience—Provincial Reconstruction Teams (PRTs)

The PRT is an example of the U.S. effort to create a nexus of civil military cooperation in a non-permissive foreign environment at the tactical level. The teams in Afghanistan, originally called Regional Teams, were a joint venture by the Afghan Government and the Coalition Military. The idea was to create civil-military cooperation centers outside the capital in each province that could accomplish three missions for the fledgling government: strengthen the reach of the Afghan central government; enhance security; and facilitate reconstruction. These three missions have been enshrined in DOD policy and approved by the Deputies and most recently were included in the adopted Terms of Reference (TOR) by the Afghan PRT Executive Steering Committee. Prior to the existence of the TOR, PRTs received little other guidance and proceeded to create their own composition and specific mission profiles within the broad guidance. To date, there are 19 PRTs including those run by other non-coalition international partners, each with their own composition of civilian and military expertise ranging in size from 60 in the U.S. sector to over 370 in the German sector. The U.S.-led PRTs have only a smattering of interagency representation, including DOS, USAID, and the Department of Agriculture. They are run by the U.S. military and are 97 percent military in composition. The IO/NGO community remains concerned by what they consider to be an encroachment of PRT mission profiles beyond the traditional security and immediate Civil Affairs quick impact assistance programs.

The relationship between these two communities is still a subject of debate, but the PRTs have moved away from small-scale activities competing with NGO projects to larger-scale projects, such as providing assistance and civil-military coordination for police; Disarmament, Demobilization and Reintegration (DDR); election support; security activities; and other functions beyond usual civil affairs activities. The PRTs have, in some cases, become essential anchors for Afghan government activities in the provinces. As the situation is evolving, it is not clear exactly how or whether the PRTs will expand their roles from missions such as elections support to involving themselves in more controversial issues such as counter narcotics (CN) operations.

Notwithstanding the need for coordinated action in such areas as CN, the issues are further exacerbated by the lack of standardization in both structure and political purpose of the PRT vis-à-vis each contributing nation. The PRTs have served as a base for International Security Assistance Force (ISAF)/NATO expansion out of Kabul, enabling U.S. forces to redeploy. However, some still think that in the end, the PRT may be seen by many as trying to be too many things to too many different stakeholders with diverging agendas.[16]

In 2004 there was a major improvement in interagency and international coordination when the Combined Forces Commander moved into the U.S. Embassy in Kabul where he was in much closer contact with the U.S. Ambassador, ISAF/NATO Commander, the UN Special Representative, and the Afghan government.

Iraq Experience

Within 60 days of the declared end of major combat action in Iraq, the United States moved to strengthen its efforts at S&R. AMB L. Paul Bremer III was appointed Presidential Envoy to Iraq to replace General Garner as the head of S&R efforts. In contrast to his predecessor, Ambassador Bremer had considerable support at the NSC, and although his reporting chain was to the Secretary of Defense, he consistently briefed the NSC and the President. Ambassador Bremer was provided considerable military support, including many members of his S&R staff. Military counterinsurgency operations and the hunt for Saddam Hussein continued to take priority for Ambassador Bremer's counterpart, LTG Ricardo S. Sanchez, Commander Multi-National Forces Iraq. General Sanchez and his ground force faced a growing military campaign that limited their engagement in S&R work. Interagency collaboration in Washington continued to be filtered through the Pentagon, which found itself stretched in managing the political build-up of a post-Saddam government concurrent with an unexpected high and growing level of insurgent activity. During this time military operations were still focused on combat operations while the civilian staff under Ambassador Bremer was focused on post conflict operations. There were some inherent crosscurrents in this situation though, overall, progress was achieved with the on-schedule turn over of authority to interim Iraqi leaders.

Soon after the transfer of authority in June 2004, AMB John D. Negroponte succeeded Ambassador Bremer and General Sanchez was replaced by GEN George W. Casey, Jr. Concurrent with these leadership changes, responsibility for reconstruction was transferred from DOD to DOS. Ambassador Negroponte followed the traditional lines of ambassadors and reported to the Secretary of State. A key feature of this new leadership was that neither Ambassador Negroponte nor General Casey worked for the other and both reported to their respective secretaries. Their offices were co-located and they placed a premium upon close cooperation between themselves and their staffs. These efforts raised the profile of the interagency process and helped reengage Washington on a broader front. On-the-ground cooperation was supported by direct links to agencies in Washington. General Casey and Ambassador Negroponte proved to be good teammates in working together on the ground. This relationship and the new lines of responsibility were supported by military progress in eliminating insurgents and civilian progress in rebuilding civil institutions along with forward momentum in the election process.

---

[16] LTC Robert Polk, Afghan Reachback Office. Email interview, February 2005.

Outside Baghdad, formal structures were established for civilian military coordination, extending the cooperation in Baghdad between the Ambassador and the Commander.

USAID Disaster Assistance Response Teams (DARTs)[17]

USAID/Office of Foreign Disaster Assistance (OFDA) deploys short and long term field personnel to countries where disasters are occurring or threaten to occur and in some cases dispatches a DART. A DART provides rapid response assistance to international disasters, as well as an operational presence on the ground with the capability to carry out sustained response activities. A DART normally includes specialists trained in a variety of disaster relief skills who assist the management of USG on-the-ground relief activities. They are now expanding into areas such as governance, elections, rule of law, and humanitarian relief. DART teams normally work closely with military civil affairs units. The structure of a DART depends on the size, complexity, type, and location of the situation and is composed of six functional areas: management/liaison; operations; planning; logistics; administration; and contracting.

For example, in Iraq, USAID recruited and trained the largest DART in U.S. history. Headquartered in Kuwait City, it had four mobile field offices. The DART was comprised of more than 70 humanitarian response experts from USAID; the DOS Bureau for Population, Migration, and Refugees; and the Department of Health and Human Service Public Health Service. In addition to technical experts in areas such as health, food, water, and shelter, the DART had statutory grant making authority and included administrative officers in logistics, transportation, and procurement, enabling the team to function as a turnkey response mechanism for assessment and funding in the field for operations in education and other reconstruction activities, going well beyond relief. In the region, the DART served as a central point of contact for USG humanitarian operations, facilitating the exchange of information and assisting in the coordination of humanitarian assistance among NGOs, UN agencies, IOs, and the U.S. military.

Civil-Military Operations Center (CMOC)[18]

The CMOC is an operational entity used ideally in peace operations and conflict and post-conflict situations such as Haiti, Bosnia, Kosovo, Iraq, and Afghanistan. Its main function is to coordinate U.S. and multinational forces humanitarian operations with local government, IOs, and NGOs who desire coordination with the military. A CMOC is usually led by U.S. Army Civil Affairs and works for the operational commander, acting as a single point of contact for civilian-related activities. It provides interface with DOS and USAID and coordinates relief efforts with U.S. and allied military commands as well as UN and other nonmilitary agencies. A CMOC also can assist in the transfer of

---

[17] U.S. Agency for International Development, "Field Operations Guide for Disaster Assessment and Response." Available online at: <http://www.usaid.gov/policy/ads/200/fog_v3.pdf >. Telephone interview with Michael Marx, Disaster Response Team Leader, Office of US Foreign Disaster Assistance, USAID, Washington, DC, April 2005.
[18] Civil Affairs Operations, Field Manual No. 41-10. Headquarters, Department of the Army, (Washington: DC, February 2000).

authority and handoff of operations from U.S. military forces to the DOS or other nonmilitary control. In Afghanistan, for example, CMOCs are found at the operational level (Kabul) and at the tactical level (provinces).

Proposed Efforts

S/CRS Model

The most forward elements of the S/CRS model would be the Advance Civilian Teams (ACTs). An ACT Integration Cell would deploy and co-locate with the military JTF headquarters and form the core of the permanent civilian S&R presence. The ACT headquarters element and the military command would join together as an EXCOM to coordinate civil-military activities on S&R. The ACT headquarters element also would oversee and support subordinate ACTs that would deploy with each brigade in support of S&R operations. Some key tasks would be to take requests for additional ACTs by military units, identify locations and priorities, resolve conflicts with military operations, coordinate support, synchronize operations with military Civil Affairs units and coordinate with the HRST. The multiple tactical ACTs operating with military brigades would deploy forward under military security and logistical support to provide direct humanitarian assistance and assist in restarting basic services, government institutions, and the local economy. Each ACT may include up to 20 personnel with requisite expertise.

CSIS Model

At the tactical level, the CSIS model establishes an Interagency Task Force (IATF) to achieve greater unity of effort in interagency operations in the field. The IATF would be created at the outset of an operation, but would not assume the lead from the COCOM until major combat operations were completed in a given area. The IATF would be led by a senior civilian Presidential-appointee, either a PSR or the U.S. Ambassador, who would report to the President through the National Security Adviser. The Combined Joint Task Force (CJTF) for S&R operations[19] would be dual-hatted as the PSR Deputy and the COCOM lead military commander on the ground for S&R operations. He or she would maintain command and control over all military forces in the area of operation. The PSR and CJTF would be supported by a fully integrated civil-military staff organized along functional lines, such as intelligence, planning, operations, and logistics. If disagreements over policy or execution could not be resolved within the IATF, the NSC process would remain the "court of appeals." The CSIS model endorses the creation of a $350 to 400 million S&R Fund that could be dispersed by the PSR to jump-start S&R projects on the ground.

---

[19] The CSIS model envisions one CJTF for Major Combat Operations and a separate CJTF for S&R operations. As major combat operations are completed in a given area, command of military operations in that area would be handed off from the CJTF MCO to the CJTF S&R. At the same time, overall lead responsibility for interagency operations in that area would be transitioned from the COCOM to the senior civilian in charge of the IATF.

Super POLAD Model

Also within the Super POLAD model is a field deployable component—the Civil-Military Action Cell (CMAC)—which would report to the COCOM through the Super POLAD. The CMAC raises the profile and expands the representation within the CMOC described under current military doctrine. The CMAC is a military provided and supported operating center for the representatives of all NGOs and IOs, as well as representatives of local government institutions and all major contractors. The CMAC is a secure entity separate from the COCOM S&R military operations center. It provides communications and information resources to its members via non-military networks. Based on need, members of the interagency may operate out of both the POLAD staff and the CMAC, however the two report independently to the S&R commander. The objective is to provide direct, participatory links to *all* players throughout the S&R process.

Ultimately, as the S&R mission succeeds, the situational exigencies that require military command will yield to conditions that allow a shift to the democratic principle of civilian leadership. Each crisis will be different. However, in the Super POLAD model it is envisaged that at an agreed time the United States will shift overall leadership responsibility from the COCOM to a U.S. diplomat, for example its ambassador to the newly formed civil leadership of the host country. When the shift in leadership occurs is less important to the model than to underscore that a restoration of normalcy includes a return to the primacy of diplomatic over military representation in bilateral relations. The transition is likely to occur when the S&R mission will have settled into a long-term phase devoid of significant military security problems. The role of the Super POLAD as well as much of the CMAC function will transfer to the diplomatic staff as the role of the COCOM reverts to peacetime military-to-military activities.

DSB Model

In addition to the contingency planning and integration task forces at the strategic level, the DSB model proposes creating a complementary joint interagency task force to ensure coordination and integration of all in-country U.S. players. The joint interagency task force would be composed of leaders of the various departments and agencies operating in a particular country of interest, to include the ambassador, station chief, USAID chief, and others. The regional combatant commander would connect to both task forces through the DOD representative.

The final component of this model is a national center for contingency support. This piece would augment the two task forces when necessary, provide a range of capability, and support planning for agencies and COCOMs.

<u>Federal Emergency Management Agency (FEMA)-like Model</u>[20]

A FEMA disaster response model holds interest because it is well-proven. FEMA uses a single scaleable organizational design for all response situations. The FEMA Emergency Response Team (ERT) is almost identical to the military staff model (four major staff sectors for personnel, intelligence, operations and logistics plus smaller special staffs for legal, medical, communications, engineers and similar competencies) formed from a combination of full time FEMA employees and part time Disaster Assistance Employees.

Teams are organized into each of the major response skill sets and sized to meet the scale of response needed. Contractor personnel are added depending on need and specialty skills, such as water treatment plant operation. A FEMA Coordination Officer (FCO) heads the ERT.

DOD provides a Defense Coordinating Officer (DCO) and a Defense Coordination Element (DCE) only when there is an immediate need such as life-saving operations and emergency sheltering or water purification requirements. The DCE deploys only as long as necessary—rarely long term. Corps of Engineer support is direct and outside the DCE. Interagency coordination is extensive (historically up to 26 agencies) and the ERT deploys its own logistics, communications, and information technology support.

---

[20] Suggested to AMB Pasqual by Army Chief of Staff GEN Peter Schoomaker on January 25, 2005. As outlined to authors by a FEMA Disaster Response Team leader. Reference for the FEMA model is the National Response Plan, December 2004. Available online at: <http://www.dhs.gov/interweb/assetlibrary/NRP_FullText.pdf>.

Conclusion

While the Pentagon debates the usefulness of the traditional 1-4-2-1 strategy in the post 9/11 environment for the current QDR, what it will be looking for is a better balance among domestic defense needs, the antiterrorism campaign, and conventional military requirements.[21] As part of this effort, DOD is "working to make stability operations a core competency of our armed forces."[22] The interagency must also adapt to the post 9/11 environment to address antiterrorism activities as well as the prolonged commitments that have evolved from the conventional wars in Afghanistan and in Iraq. Organizing the interagency to fully unite the talents of all the executive agencies for complex contingencies will alleviate the burden on our military. More and more our military forces are left dealing with the bulk of stability and reconstruction operations and "the lack of trained and deployable civilians" is a critical limiting factor in the ability of the USG to conduct S&R missions.[23]

This paper described the known models for interagency cooperation and coordination of stabilization and reconstruction operations, those which actually exist and those which are in various stages of concept development and implementation. Of these, only the S/CRS model has a conceptual structure that addresses national policy and strategy through tactical level implementation. It has Congressional support and the support of OSD, AID, and JCS.[24] The extent to which it is supported by the administration and by other agencies within the interagency is less clear. Today, it remains a concept with very little operational thrust. S/CRS lacks the resources to implement its conceptual infrastructure at the operational and tactical levels and indeed is only resourced to support a skeleton organization at the national level and further develop its overall structure and vision. The creation of S/CRS is a catalyst to organizing the State Department and AID better for rapid response in times of crisis. The notion of an Active Reserve Corps if funded will allow the DOS to quickly establish or increase diplomatic presence on the ground from its cadre of foreign and civil service officers. According to June 16, 2005 testimony, S/CRS staff include AID, OSD, JCS, JFC, Corps of Engineers, Department of Treasury and Intel community staff. Remove the military components and the level of interagency representation is marginal.[25]

There is common agreement that the USG must move to resolve its current capability deficiency in S&R as soon as possible. The solution to this capability deficiency lies in

---

[21] Thom Shanker and Eric Schmitt, "Pentagon Weighs Strategy Change to Deter Terror," *The New York Times*, July 5, 2005.

[22] Ryan Henry, Principal Deputy Under Secretary of Defense for Policy. "Prepared Statement for the Senate Foreign Relations Committee, June 16, 2005." Available online at: <http://foreign.senate.gov/hearings/2005/hrg050616a.html>.

[23] Ibid

[24] Please see prepared statements from the Senate Foreign Relations Committee held a hearing on June 16, 2005, on "Stabilization and Reconstruction: Building Peace in a Hostile Environment" for more information. These are available online at: <http://foreign.senate.gov/hearings/2005/hrg050616a.html>.

[25] Ambassador Carlos Pascual, Coordinator for Reconstruction and Stabilization. Prepared Statement for the Senate Foreign Relations Committee, June 16, 2005.

the interagency and not in any one department alone. In fact, the USG does not need to undertake this deficiency on its own but should take advantage of the capabilities of international organizations such as the AU and NATO. None of the models fully integrate this idea. Within the USG, the departments will all face challenges to their institutional identity and culture as none of them, other than AID and Treasury, is currently organized to respond to complex contingency requirements. Regardless of the model that is followed, existing elements should be incorporated into new organizational structures, and ad hoc responses to crises should no longer be the norm. A change in the institutional paradigm of the USG is required to assign a new and much higher priority to capacity for interagency integration and coordination over the traditional functions of individual departments. It is entirely possible that, in addition to changes which will be needed to authorize and allocate resources to implement S/CRS, consideration should be given to a form of "Goldwater-Nichols for the interagency" to bring jointness to the interagency in a manner analogous to that in which Goldwater-Nichols brought jointness to the military departments in the mid-1980s.

At a minimum, the following would help interagency collaboration and coordination:

- A bargain between DOD and civilian agencies in which civilian agencies agree to participate in complex operations and the Defense Department agrees to help provide them with the capacity to do so.
- A National Security Policy Directive that broadly addresses complex operations and the roles and responsibilities of executive agencies in such contingencies.
- Resources to make S/CRS an operational and tactical entity.
- Resources to expand the JIACGs into real interagency planning and operational organizations.
- Strategic leadership for complex operations at the NSC-level.
- Integration of existing elements such as the Army's Civil Affairs units, AID's DART, DOD's JIACG into any new concepts avoiding the creation of duplicative organizations.
- Unity of command through coordinated civilian and military leadership in the field.
- Integration of international resources into complex contingency planning and operations.